The American Poetry Review/ Honickman First Book Prize

The Honickman Foundation is dedicated to the support of projects that promote spiritual growth and creativity, education and social change. At the heart of the mission of the Honickman Foundation is the belief that creativity enriches contemporary society because the arts are powerful tools for enlightenment, equity and empowerment, and must be encouraged to effect social change as well as personal growth. A current focus is on the particular power of photography and poetry to reflect and interpret reality, and, hence, to illuminate all that is true.

The annual American Poetry Review/Honickman First Book Prize offers publication of a book of poems, a $3,000 award, and distribution by Copper Canyon Press through Consortium. Each year a distinguished poet is chosen to judge the prize and write an introduction to the winning book. The purpose of the prize is to encourage excellence in poetry, and to provide a wide readership for a deserving first book of poems. *Rhinoceros* is the seventh book in the series.

Winners of The American Poetry Review/ Honickman First Book Prize

Joshua Beckman *Things Are Happening* 1998

Dana Levin *In the Surgical Theatre* 1999

Anne Marie Macari *Ivory Cradle* 2000

Ed Pavlić *Paraph of Bone & Other Kinds of Blue* 2001

Kathleen Ossip *The Search Engine* 2002

James McCorkle *Evidences* 2003

Kevin Ducey *Rhinoceros* 2004

Rhinoceros

Rhinoceros

poems

Kevin Ducey

Winner of The APR/Honickman First Book Prize

The American Poetry Review

Philadelphia

Distribution by Copper Canyon Press/Consortium.

Library of Congress Control Number: 2004103258

ISBN 0-9718981-5-4 (cloth, alk. paper)
ISBN 0-9718981-6-2 (pbk., alk. paper)

First edition
Designed by Adrianne Onderdonk Dudden
Composed by Duke & Company

Acknowledgments
The following poems have previously appeared:
"Wheels" and "Spirit Guide" in *Malahat Review;* "Wim Wenders vs. the Wolfman"
and "Dien Bien Phu" in *Crab Orchard Review;* "No Distance" in *Puerto del Sol;*
"Far off in a field once" in *Fox Cry Review;* "Hawking and Disney take lunch" in *Elixir 3;*
"The Bridge" in *Samizdat.*

For Bridget

In Memoriam:
Tim Breakfast Wunderlin

" . . . *che ci affliggono i disiri*
e li altri affetti, l'ombra si figura;
equest' è la cagion di che tu miri."
—Dante, *Purgatorio* XXV

"*as we are plagued by desire*
and appetite, so are we figured in that shadow;
here's the pathology of what you've seen."

Contents

V

VI

Foreword

Kevin Ducey's *Rhinoceros* has a playfulness that pulses alongside a seriousness, and this rippling effect resonates beneath the skin. There's a controlled singing at the center of each poem; and yet, the verbal leaps and flashes suggest a willingness to let language seek its own unwinding and spiritual depth. The reader is drawn into these seemingly straightforward lyrical narratives, but soon one realizes that the twists and turns are not simple. In fact, this seduction begins with the first section of the book's first poem "Dien Bien Phu":

> He had gone
> (one chieftain to another)
> carrying his flintlock.
>
> The secret service agents
> hadn't noticed until
> he was finishing
> the nickel tour of
> the East Wing.
>   The French
> called them Meo, or sometimes
> Yeo—they being so unprepossessing
> they didn't bother to
> correct the name.

So, from the onset, we learn that a keen imagination drives these impressive poems. Many first books are populated with narratives about family, friends, and place—personal and social histories that seem rather myopic. *Rhinoceros* is multifaceted, a merger of so-called high and low cultures. The observed and imaginary become one; and, of course, this seamlessness coheres through tone.

And, when the reader arrives at the book's end, the last stanza of "Wim Wenders vs. the Wolfman," one realizes the importance of the journey:

The angels of the lord stop by.
They are terrible
in their changeless desire.
They're on their way
to blast Sodom and want
a coffee and a fag. You don't smoke
and only have de-caf.
Surely, the Lord will smite you down—
if only you knew it.
                    Your angels insist
they don't want any bread, so
you give them oranges—feeling
your eyebrows singe as they
take them from your hands.
In this fire, you recognize
here is something outside the human:
a fulcrum that would move planets.

Indeed, *Rhinoceros*'s compass points us "outside the human" so that
we may plot and map internal terrain. History and philosophy collide
with popular culture, and a tension is created that the mind and body
understand simultaneously. Images drift into each other till words multiply
through signification—in this world and otherworldly. In other words,
the planets in *Rhinoceros* are not fixed or stationary, and there are shifting
definitions and perspectives throughout this marvelous first collection.

Most first books are a hodgepodge, but Ducey's collection possesses a
planned trajectory, a calibrated velocity of controlled feelings. The tonal
certainty of these poems underlines the shape of a mature vision. There's al-
most a scientific, studied quality of observation—a matter-of-factness
that renders authority, where even the moments of abstraction have meat
on the bone. The imaginative is taken as a belief system, as gospel, as
possibility.

With lyrical turns and metaphorical sways, *Rhinoceros* embodies mythologies that are brought down to earth, and one can feel the power of a masterful signifier. The sacred bleeds into the profaned, and boundaries grow almost invisible. A cogent example of this skilled playfulness is in "Homo Habilis":

> I saw a wooly rhinoceros yesterday
> and we chased it down to the Stop'n Rob.
> Edmond killed it, but we were too far
> from the cave to get it back home
> before nightfall and the hyenas.
>
> We give each other drill bits
> for Christmas. We don't really like
> each other, but a tool is always
> appreciated. A pack of angels
> from the main office came down—
> wanted to see how things were working
> out. How we were getting along.
> They ignored Edmond and his
> fancy talk about astronomy, but they
> fluffed their wings over my new drill bits.
> "Atta boy," they said. "Nice tool." So we
> showed them what we'd been making.
> Carol brought out her toothpick; Sy,
> his business card holder. The angels
> nodded to each other
> making marks in things they called 'books.'
>
> Then Susan had to wreck it all. She told them
> of the death of her child—the little girl
> we were all so fond of and
> the terrible accident of her death.
> "This sorrow is my tool—sharpened

so hard and close to my heart,"
she said to the head angel.
"I don't need a stone to sharpen it,
this blade never grows dull. It is with me
always, never far
never far from my hand. Do you see?
Do you see its fine, sharp edge?" The angels
shook their heads. Closing their books,
they said, "here is one we don't know.
How quick it cuts, how sharp the blade." They backed
from our cave as if afraid. At the door, the last one paused,
his wings, we now noticed, looked a little worse for wear,
"from here out," he said, "you suckers are on your own."

With a tough-hewn horn, a weapon displayed on the crown of its head,
this is nobody's fallen unicorn. *Rhinoceros* is robust, sturdy as an ox, and
it stands on its own ground. Get ready for a rewarding duel.

Yusef Komunyakaa
2004

Rhinoceros

Dien Bien Phu

The danger of dualist religions . . . is potential reversion to polytheism, to multiple and local gods, always a threat to Imperium. What follows in the name of the Word is Crusade, Auto-da-Fé, religious war . . .

—*A Gathering of Proper Names*, Brooke Bergan

1.

He had gone
(one chieftain to another)
carrying his flintlock.

The secret service agents
hadn't noticed until
he was finishing
the nickel tour of
the East Wing.
        The French
called them Meo, or sometimes
Yeo—they being so unprepossessing
they didn't bother to
correct the name.

2.

A river winds through
the fortress and at night
during the siege
we could always go down
to trade with the Greeks.
How else
to maintain this uneasy war?
        Ten thousand
deserters have settled here
this narrow zone

of the Scamander or Nam Yum.
They've put up tents, dug
caves, sell food
from the black market—stuff
we can't get up on the walls.
Many of us still in retreat
from Stalingrad, avoiding
an interview with Weisenthal.

3.
The Vandals beyond the Rhine
were largely runaway slaves, dispossessed
freemen, seniors
unable to afford
prescription drugs—
Rome had it coming.

The old poet implied things
might change and ended
under a helmet on the walls
of Tomis on the Black Sea.

> His sergeant:
> Those hooligans out there, pal,
> don't care much for your poetry—
> They zooming round in them
> shaggy pony chariots (celts?) with
> .50 caliber mounted on back. Go
> tell it to the Geats.

(Though Ovid did
grow fond of the people of Tomis,
learned their depraved

tongue and before he
died wrote a few poems in that
Greekish.

"You gotta live w/
yr people
as well as yr ghosts."

She liked
these American things we sold
out of the shop
on Steinentor Strasse. We
went for a drink
across from the LälleKönig.
I love you Americans, she said.
You're so happy; no
sense of history.

4.

The back of the panel truck
rattled open at the farmers' market
in Minneapolis and the press
of Hmong shoppers
pushed me forward. The truck
was full of some fresh, green plant.
Something I'd never
noticed before, long stalk, with
single leaf—shaped
like an ancient spear-head. They
were tied in bunches and the people
all around me waved their dollars
shouting out their need.

Was it ceremonial? I tried to imagine
an American plant I'd desire as much.
A French-fry? The particular is
what you eat. The old
cheesemakers of Gloucestershire
can say which side of the hill
brings the best milk.
                    (Though
cheese was not always so sedentary—
it was Odin's food, the nomad's accident
of milk
carried from the Rhine crossing to
Augustine's city.
                    Only
here could someone say, 'I don't care
about food.' Or, as the meat inspector
said on resigning: I don't care
if it is irradiated, it's still shit.

Hero Tales

1. Restoration Tragedy

The King has entered. The
ladies and gentlemen
flutter once
before resettling in their
seats as his majesty
takes a place on stage
(down right). He extends
his perfumed, scabrous
arm to the hero
of our piece and asks:
'bite me, please.'

If memory serves,
I'd recognize this as a
habitual tic.
                    Likewise,
it's the way someone's
absence stays with you: a
presence,
           you turn
a corner
for instance
(Mary) into a city
of absence wherever you are.
To be fair,
you inhabit others' lives
as only the negative
image of their loss—

7

the opaque orange
counter-image of a life
colored   elsewhere.

2. Atalanta/Batman

Under the full moon
the sense of a poem
came over me:
something heroic—
though I resisted the
impulse and stayed away
from all things Kerouac.

At first light I saw
someone had cut cropcircles
in my new bonsai.

The heroes arrived
and took it back
to the Batcave.
'Medusawork,' the Batman
said. 'You see the poet
frozen in an aspect
of desire.
The creature clearly
wanted to look away.'

'What pornography
of hope is this,
Batman!' The Boy
Wonder says
(oh yes, yes he does).

But later that night
after the Batman inadvertently
revealed to Robin that the secret
of their origins
lay in a Ukrainian shtetl,
Robin, now the Boy
Verklemmt (overtaken like
Atalanta in the
catastrophe of history) felt
a certain chill.
              The Batmitzvahman
(hoping to relieve the
cold melancholy) doused
the Bonsai in gasoline and
set it afire, saying:
'but look, this
poem here for instance . . .'

Over and After

" . . . it seems we must be brought hard up against the unlovely body
of Aesthetics."

—G. Hill, *The Triumph of Love*

Such a perception of an unformed thing
might bring you to laughter. Beauty
sold for a few catch-words. It's easy
enough to do: a hunchback, a dwarf-
spirit caught in the right glass
might cast a finer shadow. e.g.
the Aliotorous Res. It's hard enough
working the poem when it's continually
misplaced: double that when it
misplaces me and goes on alone.
There's the comedic, I'll have us back
on track in a moment, I'm still
climbing from the tar. Oh, blackest
eyes wrest from me these routines:
the set-up, wait a moment, I'll remember
the punch-line. It comes in threes
ba da da-da da Dah. I flung
open the door to find the archaic
fucking the dead (no, don't go there)
both screaming. Went home wistful.

The digging—so many
                    exhumations
of the body   my own   I own—
[ba da da-da da] dumped by
the gangster at a building site.
Has reader in such manner ever
been wooed? Wait for it:

Patrons are hereby advised
to go and catch a falling starre—
go and sew it to your clothes.
                          Permanent
revolution played out as a gentle
continuous mugging. That cudgel
quaint and archaic
doubles as a fulcrum to shove the world.

In the end that's beginning
they meet cute:
                  the boy pauses
to pick up that bauble of gold
(a tooth filling?) and the
Angel of History—head turned
back in dismay—
                        trips over
                        the fool.

Body Stalking

seems to me she is wrong to designate the nonlexical . . .
　　　　　　　　　—Charles Bernstein, *A Poetics*

[1.
So much depends . . .

The sort of word that throws
you forward:
　　　　　es hängt
it's hanging (a scaffold)
future
　　　pending
At the time when WCW
wrote
　　　things
were pending
　　　　　pendeln
　　　　　to swing in transition
and the language
truly spoken by men
(if it can be said
they speak) best caught
with instrument
stripped to Depression
era lean-ness to navigate
the century—
　　　　　　if there
is still a future hanging—
you leave the speaking
to your credit card.
I'll need a language
big as my car, a huge

15

new house set on a
postage stamp, an extra
genetic eye big enough
to see it.   ]

. . . pointing at the beyond domain tentacle
to hug pataphysical. A hug us
(us in here)
even some of my friends
within interstitial platforms
made real by formal configurations/chat
girl-talk eating, as
perforce, hegemony-
flavored ice-creams some dynamic
some withstood (as my friends in St. Tropez)
only vibrant part
that is 'real.' She extruding
in a systematic way
made clear in conference
read paper in St. Tropez the
Ultimate Journal at her stoops,
the gaze, you recline, we speak 'du'
as Lévi-Strauss in a parallel paper to this
my poem
has discovered the lycantropic woven
in mattresses throughout European fucking. I am not
say, for refusal, the most vibrant part
that is 'the real' (not the 'real'). She, extruding,
liberates 'hibit' from ex
and unlocks the aperçus: lingual
hermeneutics ensue.

Julia,
as we know, only factitiously liquifacts
refusing to be absorbed she

liquidates the porifera
of the inert and lobotomized
in a form of camp, point at
say, Mandelstam, paralleling
my work looking at only
at only a blue sky.
Perhaps outlined better in
clarified limited range of finger battalions
she stops. Though she stops. Not breath:
Body stockings, as performed
in paper by Bob in St. Tropez.
Meaning transferred in fluid
comfort, or moved into
the errata: p. 61, l. 33 pointed not pointing
        p. 113, l. 6 still not stills
        p. 186, l. 31 suppresses not supresses
        p. 188, l. 2 surprise not suprise
        p. 257, l. 16 indent
        p. 260, l. 16 indent
The errata rolled in Persian rugs, first we
hot-pluggable. Ports automatically
recognized and installed: peripherals roll
and apply lubricant for rapt presentness
we squeegee lotion coating tongue teeth vocable . . .

Tottering Rats

And so they said that these matters bee Kynges games, as it were stage playes,
and for the most part plaied upon scafoldes . . .

The History of King Richard The Third, Sir Thomas More,
quoted in The Nonconformist's Memorial, Susan Howe

I.

Mary found the
Garden, full of
gardeners busy
moving bodies about.

She turned herself
They spread
out a blanket and lunch,
fried animal parts,
parts formed in loaves.
Mary was standing
where the swallows flew
where Melville in Jerusalem,
Shiloh
      left sand in the sandwiches
Wingate flew in, too,
with a chindit in his teeth:
"not that big of a loaf
after all, to chase the Italians
out of Ethiopia," he said.
Pelicans build their nests
in the portmanteaus of
earlier traditions of mud,
errata . . .
      Gardener has the body
in Jerusalem, turn left

after the fourth Zoa.
Rough trade, Trust: He went to
ask the gardener/Con man.

Then the note arrived:

He ran off leaving his rake.

Julian in her cave—

always someone knocking

at the little window

looking for a rat

poem: something

to keep the English
Delayed again

out.
some flight

      We are the English.
midnightly

Rats.
mute why

not say love where in May

cornets in 'D'

A ghost of the son
(in White Jacket the exile
remembers actions, but as
a shadow).

Knew he'd kill
before he'd take a flogging—
calculating the distance to
the ship's side—as it happened:

        I answered the phone.
        —I called to tell you
        your father died.

        Oh, ma, how—

This morning, I came
home and he was on the couch
as usual, but not moving.

Christ, Jesus,
I don't know—

I don't know either, but he's
sitting up now, why don't I let him
tell you about it.

Well, hello there—

But, she said you were dead—

Well, yes. But that doesn't mean
I can't still call, does it?

■   ■   ■

Some hunger, some carry
letters from Ma'aara—severed
heads the Crusaders
catapulted over the walls

Melville clerked in customs.
Isaac Babel: "I declined
to become a clerk."
Stalin saw to that—
a good deal of
volumes done up in
dust floating in Odessa,
Charity, love? Like a glass

of water. The wit
in the Comintern:
"I want a clean glass."
                              None
flew to Parnassus.

We drug him along
the lightning killed him
on the third tee,
but we finished the round.
The shadow
Christ took with him in death
for example
Lazarus not
exactly happy to be
back in harness.

A shadow visit to hell where
Coyote can't restrain himself
this place where we keep circling
around. A waltz better than
a hymn and all our ironies
of bitter elegy.

Double stress   double shadow
body moves   the corporeal
who was the gardener?
with Arimathea hovering—
another contributing
sponsor: give him a brick
with his name on it.
Hard time for the word
when it's a Brick. There's little use

in a noun and when He
showed up back at the
ranch, He must've been pure Verb.

II. The Argument
Richard III (the play) was popular
in Cromwell's New Model Army—
the story of an unpopular
usurper carried forward on a hod
of bricks
        electoral fraud
and the hope of getting Charles I
on a Bosworth field screaming for a horse
more dramatic, but less dignified than
a quiet prayer on the scaffold.

     "I have only a few
     words: loiter
     redeemable
     Coupon
     Tender
     Sock
     grapefruit
     Lick.
     I haven't yet seen that movie everyone is talking about. I remember
     the first time I asked about flan. My rodeos were always hot; my rain
     wet.   wet.   wet.
     I don't ever
     want to be
     French.   I cried for shame.
     Sometimes I felt shame before my dog. A very good dog. My tomb
     was more thought on than my bedroom. Is this color all right on me?
     Is there more of that fine American nostrum 'tobacco'? My dukes

Buckingham,York and Oxford plague me with loaves. Meat.
I mean
loaves of meat. I enjoy,
most of all, when Mistress Joist
sprinkles corn across my
naked body and the chickens
pluck it all away. Let us put down
all false porcelains; it will make us
Dutch. Dis—ah, I mean—Re-member."

III.
Lake Titicaca bibliography
of the con: Fidelé.
                    In the holy land
a certain hazy transcendence settled over
his head (after which he wrote *Billy*).

The tongue
drags the body after.

King Richard (the other one)
chased Saladín through
Hebron, Acre, Tyre—
desiring a photo op.
                    Saladín
replying with scorn
he saw no reason
to parley with the English
while they were there
in arms. (Michael Palaeologous
took the meeting).

Those iconoclasts closed the theaters
even though the New Model Army
played Richard III throughout Ireland:
"How stands our tottering state?"

Where the great king—a crumbling stone
edifice carved into the mountainside
(explosives set like Martin Marprelate
with printing presses across the countryside
wingéd tongues flying like Quarles tiny puns)—
falls.

Rhinoceros Quick Tongue Absence

Among the heaps of brick and plaster lies
a girder, still itself among the rubbish.
            —Charles Reznikoff

After one of his usual absences
the entry into the city:

the first imperative: avoid
being eaten. Fear of eating . . .

"breakfasted this morning
on rhinoceros hump . . . "

. . . one's relatives, or the
God. An organ, possessed
by man and most vertebrates,
occupying the floor of the
mouth . . .

            The lord, looking
about the great hall when the people
had all assembled, noticed one
in no festiual frok, bot fyled with werkkez.

'Say me frende,' quoth the freke
with a felle chere, 'How wan thou
into this won in wedez so fowle?'

Michael Rockefeller had no answer. The
goat with a crown of laurel led to the
Lord's dungeon for preparation . . .

A mouth of quick brimstone
—and the tiny dead bodies
piling up in the Stromatolite
Diorama in Chicago.

Yet you shall be sure to raise up the quick earth
which had not been stirred up with the Plough before.

For his [Charles II's] long absence
Church and State did groan.
                              It is tapering,
blunt-tipped, muscular, soft and fleshy,
important in taking in food.

                    Mrs. Wheeler (1821): Wor thor
                    giants alive?   Mary: Nay,
                    nay . . . they er net whick I racken.

Goddes heste, that heet the erthe
brynge forthe gras and quyk bestes

Crist fastide fourty daies . . . he was
in quyke age, and listede wel to ete.

                    Gower *Conf* III 143. 1390:
              There schal a worthi king
              beginne to kepe his tunge
              and to be trewe.
                        The entry
              of any king into a city
              is the image of Christ's advent
              in Jerusalem—Richard II's
              for instance in 1392 (even greeted

by John the Baptist [Richard's
particular saint] who, pointing
out the King, announced:
'Behold the Lamb of God').
But in 1393, Richard was still
picking his way through
the carcasses and offal, bricks
and mortar, of Fleet Street
from Holborn to Westminster and
Richard himself then
deposed and starved in the Tower
(the butchers'
rubbish still in the gutter).

WC Baldwin *Afr Hunting* 1863 viii. 327:
I saw four rhinoceros drinking at the fountain.

The gome knew not what to answer
to kepe one's tunge, to kepe silence—
(He was so out of his mind
with confusion lest he should suffer)
"That he ne wyst on worde
what he warp schulde."

There is plenty of rhino spoor, but
we have not yet found them.

A house is a vocabulary. A city
is a language. And attached at its
base
      to the hyoid bone;
often protrusible and freely
movable.

With quickflesh contest if you need:
there is no argument with bone.

Our Lord . . . was now returning to Capernaum—
after one of his usual absences . . .

Top of the World

Is it true that words carry no promise . . .
A glittering chest, but full of ashes?
                            —Yves Bonnefoy

I

Shadows caught by nets—
shadows written in stone onto
                the mountain:
the sealed box carried across
the Channel.

Here's a Franks' Casket:
carved in runes and
riddle. These figures
(closed eyes) unsealed.

II

The father,
Liu Yide, a poor
villager living in Tantou,
says his son, Yifang, phoned home on June 14,
saying he would make the crossing to England
from Holland.

Pressed together
(closer than stones)
patents of life taken across the border.

The family paid
20,000 renminbi
to the snakehead, a further 220,000
to be paid from the son's future earnings.

III

It must once have taken
a speaker of genius
or of manic longing
to compare one's love
to the sea.

The Casket says:
The horse sits
      on the mound of woe.
           [or also read: Here the guards
              set upon Harmberga (a person)].

IV

The driver says:
he was told there were only sixteen people
in the trailer
and that the men
promised him $2,500 to take the group
to Robstown.

He says, my friends,
that he was called later on his cellular phone
and offered another $2,500
to continue to Houston.

It was north of Robstown
on Route 77 where the trapped people
began to claw at the insulation.

V

We read: 'The sea became furious
      where he (now the fish) swam ashore.'

If we were to open
that box—
        falling into silence
at midday
        here on the roadway—life
all around us streaming past—
we listen
without comprehension. Everything
is darkness. One hundred and thirty degrees
of silence. Talk to us, O vagabond,
teach us something.

Homo Habilis

The tool-maker

> *Praise the world to the angel, not the unutterable world;*
> *you cannot astonish him with your glorious feelings . . .*
>
> —R. M. Rilke, *The Duino Elegies*

I saw a wooly rhinoceros yesterday
and we chased it down to the Stop'n Rob.
Edmond killed it, but we were too far
from the cave to get it back home
before nightfall and the hyenas.

We give each other drill bits
for Christmas. We don't really like
each other, but a tool is always
appreciated. A pack of angels
from the main office came down—
wanted to see how things were working
out. How we were getting along.
They ignored Edmond and his
fancy talk about astronomy, but they
fluffed their wings over my new drill bits.
"Atta boy," they said. "Nice tool." So we
showed them what we'd been making.
Carol brought out her toothpick; Sy,
his business card holder. The angels
nodded to each other
making marks in things they called 'books.'
Then Susan had to wreck it all. She told them
of the death of her child—the little girl
we were all so fond of and
the terrible accident of her death.
"This sorrow is my tool—sharpened
so hard and close to my heart,"

she said to the head angel.
"I don't need a stone to sharpen it,
this blade never grows dull. It is with me
always, never far
never far from my hand. Do you see?
Do you see its fine, sharp edge?" The angels
shook their heads. Closing their books,
they said, "here is one we don't know.
How quick it cuts, how sharp the blade." They backed
from our cave as if afraid. At the door, the last one paused,
his wings, we now noticed, looked a little worse for wear,
"from here out," he said, "you suckers are on your own."

Far off in a field once

Far off in a field once
I chanced to see my hand
bathing in a pond.
I think it was my hand—
it had its front turned toward me.
I was astonished
to see the small, naked thing there.
So vulnerable to the world,
the hand, bathing itself,
shivered once in the autumn air.

Edison & Browning

A whisper of the cylinder
and someone is heard
in the background urging the
poet to try again.
                    I seem
to have forgotten my verses.
A small valence between
remembrance and
a passing over.
                    Mr. Browning
sneaks a glance at the other
old man in the studio, the inventor
of this scene. Edison can't hear a thing,
so he listens through his teeth.
He appears to be chewing
the woodframe of his recording
device. *I'm sorry, I seem to have*
forgotten my verses.
                        Do try another,
someone urges while the irascible
engineer gnaws at the box.
Does it matter if the teeth are
his own? Do we perceive beauty
only through the senses, or will
artifice make up the lack?
                        The assistants
were still talking about it: the week
before Edison had spat out the wood,
jumped to his feet, shouting at
Rachmaninov (mid-crescendo):
Stop that, stop. You're a pounder.
That's what you are: a pounder.

42

Hawking and Disney take lunch

For Paul

Time flattens out—
like young Stephen Hawking's wristwatch
under his waiter's heel.
Hawking taps the waiter's knee
who puts his nose deep into the air
before he goes.
                  Across the table,
Disney gives up on the conversation
and scratches out pictures of a new character.
He laughs to himself, 'a duck
in a sailor suit—now that's funny.' Hawking
grabs the paper away and on the back
of Donald Duck's afterbirth writes:
'Dear President Roosevelt—the gravity
of the situation prompts my petition.
I fear the Russians are developing
a new device called 'strip mall:'
they threaten us with
endless consumption, unless—
unless—we get there *first.*
Won't you carry me, sir, oh,
carry me like that flying goat
of Chagall?
I see it all so clear: History
as I've stopped it here
on my plate. Imagine it as
a little obelisk of potato and peas.
This drawing may resemble a duck
in a sailor suit, to you, Mr. President,

but you overlook how egg yolk
can stiffen
the farthest margin of creation's first moment.

Heretic

Immediately after we
condemned the last
of the heretics I
went downstairs to catch
the early train home.
The subway was crowded
and as the train lingered
at the platform I
thought of the white
blindfold tied 'round
the old man's face as the
judgement was read. I like
to see the children dancing
between the soldiers' lockstep—
like those tiny clock figures serving
attendance on the hours. The train
pulls out and bangs along the
underground curves, reaching
into the mountain, coming into
blazing sunlight on the other side.
Mechanical time is not
to be mistaken for life's passage
any more than this apparition of my desire
(glimpsed in an old man's gasp of fear)
is the same as that flame
that once burned so clear.

Leviathan singing

Those pebbles on the beach don't struggle for position
or do they? The whisper of the ocean may be
all the suppressed desire of an age. Though the shadows
along the beach lengthen, the ocean is louder still. I press
to my ear a seashell and hear your whisper.
It's more than our years can hold—
this desire goes back to the time when the ocean
covered all and leviathan sang over all the world. Oh, the
scientists know, looking out of their research labs as
the snow begins to fall, it will fall forever now—
one melting drop by drop. They look on the lazy,
determined falling   falling: how the earth held you once.

The Lover Speaks of Natural History

Praise to Allah for my love
is here with me tonight.
All praise to GM's biggest truck
for my love speaks my name
and doesn't waste my time.
There is no sleep
but we are together.

When all America has passed
when all the gas stations
have turned to delis
they will speak of my love for you.
And your reality has slowed and I
used to think of death as something
one practiced and the Buddha had
the simple trick of it, but your hand
is in mine, and I kiss your mouth
and it has slowed for me
as well and there is no dying
here in this place inside of a time when
the President is finally dead
and the glaciers are all tenderness.

All praise to your body that you are
inside and I hold in my arms
and these places you go when you dream,
likewise, the body then is referential.
All praise to the game of Monopoly
which is referential and
this token you leave of yourself here
in my arms when you sleep
could have been the Hat or the Dog.

Neo dolls

Archeologists disagree on the fate
of the neanderthals.
Some say our ancestors arrived
and killed them all; while
a new school believes that
the two species were not that different
and that homo sapiens showed up
because the neanderthals were babes.
Neanderthals were apparently quite friendly,
they liked romantic dinners, walks
on the beach. They were avid ice-age
dancers. What was not to like?
        We
had to wait for this discovery until
a critical mass of divorced scientists
took up the mirror of the personal ads
and traced the fate of the neanderthals
in the shifting reflections of desire.

Pearls

These are the pearls, Edison's
machine to pick up transmissions
from the dead. The dog Laika's
fading heartbeat as she orbits
the earth in her tiny Russian
capsule, the bright flower print
skirt of the woman across the way
walking unsteady as the night
the drunk woman once
in Piccadilly Circus alone
and leaning over a banister
do you need a cab, I mean, a taxi?
do you need help? Not sure
she spoke English. Not sure I did.
Robert Browning recorded by Edison
as the poet's scratchy voice
makes a slight impress on the machine.
"I'm sorry, I seem to
have forgotten my verses."
                                Well,
do try another one someone
is heard urging Mr. Browning on.
The drunk woman spat,
mumbled something and
stumbled back into the pub.
In 1969 the movie Oliver came out
and my inability to pronounce
the letter 'r' became an asset on the
playground. He's not queer,
he's the Ahtfull Dodgeh. Get him
to say 'bird.' That's a riot. How 'bout:
'can I get you a taxi?' My season
as Oliver was short-lived and if Edison's machine

was discovered behind some brick wall
would Browning's memory be any better? Or
would he whisper to us, *Oh yes, the earth,*
soul, body I once counted as my own. I have here
a coupon I meant to redeem—

Natural History Museums

When I was fifteen
I went to Denver's Natural History
Museum with Lisa Huntzecker
and her parents.
            We wandered
along the musty aisles
of dead stuffed things
and when her parents
turned a corner
she took my hand:
"I want to show you something."
And we stood in a narrow alcove,
a marble wall
pushed against my back,
a glass display case behind hers.
She took me in her arms
turned her face up to mine,
her braided hair
loitered upon her left shoulder
like a blond rodent, the soft cotton
of her purple Indian hippie shirt
slid beneath my fingertips.
"Here we are—" she said,
but we weren't alone,
I glanced up to the glass case
behind her head
into the eyes of the great barn owl,
wings spread wide, talons drawn and sharp,
beak and pointy pink tongue
fixed in endless scream.
Um, I said: um—
What is it you wanted to show me?

All my life I've taken
comfort in these long, cool museum
hallways, following the timelines—
hundreds of feet of the cenozoic,
triassic, cambrian, and at the very end,
after a few inches of the paleolithic,
the modern age labors to take root—
the barest sheen of mold on the
twenty-five-layer cake of time.
It would be a poor family's wedding
to enjoy icing so thin. The work
of our parents and their parents—
yea, to the nth generation—
is not the fullest rose of time.

Still, she was going to show
me something. The sweet trade
of a kiss against
that dark green strip of Cambrian
hunger, these millions of days,
all the aching dreams
of paleontology pressed to my back.

Viewers like me

for Mark

You mentioned the sparrows, nest building
on the window ledges
of the clinic. Comparing them to Shakespeare
constructing a sonnet line by line by husk
of grass. I wondered if
you were talking about death making its nest
in any body—apparently random, bit
by bit—some attempts fail,
but death sets up house eventually:
It may be the last comfort
life gives you.
                    Conversation or friendship
built up by the small pieces we've each carried.
Here's your old friend, the sparrow,
scratching at a window ledge. Where
did I conceal that bit of vinca I should have handed over?
Maybe it's the plug of tobacco in my mouth? Nothing
to conceal, it was there all along.

2

Yesterday the landlord came by and stopped up
the inlet by the air conditioner
where the birds came in. We asked him to do it.
Sparrows and starlings. The news
of their disagreements woke us day after day.
Starlings aren't even native—some Shakespeare
enthusiast released them and all the other species
mentioned in the plays into Central Park. (Did he hope
perhaps to influence the next playwright? That's what
American theater has always needed—more birds.)
This morning I wake and listen to their sparrow

cries and hope I'm hearing only the birds
on the outside—upset that they're locked out—
and the sounds I hear aren't from birds walled up
Edgar-Allan-Poe-like, inside the wall. (If Fortunato
had only known more and better stories
he could have avoided that final brick.

                           A lot of writers
think like that. But our conversations
are too often bereft of kindness and barely a shred of vinca
to pick up between us for an understanding.)

Video Chorus

What measure shall I give these generations
that breathe on the void and are void
And exist and do not exist?

                                              —Sophocles

In Mexico the whole family
crowded into the bedroom to watch the Challenger
on the television. The rocket
clawing at the sky
                         a bad launch like a dreamer
being chased. A moment ago you could fly over houses
and your old school and now, when the monster comes close,
your arms flap at the air and you run through mud.
"Ay yi," we sigh. Here, too, in the land
of astronomical certitude, the Aztecs and Mayans
understood this management of the heavens
as the prerogative of power. Priests
drop an o-ring into ice water to demonstrate
that the third element is not given. On the screen
the repetition begins. The rocket shakes free of the gantry,
rising into the sky and, in spite of our fore-knowledge,
we think, 'this time it will be all right,' before the thing
explodes again, death's rose on a jet stream stalk.
And before you can turn away, the rocket full of people
is again on the launch pad, ready to flower.
Comedy is only funny once, tragedy breeds compulsion.
The four officers beat the black man over and over;
The woman drives her car off the quake-shattered bridge
and then she does it again. Here are our timid tragedies
before the gods. Watching that chorus of video screens,
we know everything there is to know. We know who
the killer was on the road to Thebes,

but we'll watch it again. We'll watch it
again, to study the face of fortune's wit, thinking
this time, this time it will stop.
This time we'll render justice, find a brake pedal underfoot,
a parachute by the door.

No Distance Makes You Difficult

Keine Ferne macht dich schwerig,
Kommst geflogen und gebannt
                    —Goethe

No distance makes you difficult.
You exist always
here
you were difficult to begin—
distance had nothing to do with it.

You come flying and spell-bound.
How I would shrug this off:
Slide from under the burden,
and stand, free, beside myself.
The days before
my eyes met yours and you smiled:
how my heart flew
(when I held you) right out the door.
I held then
everything
by a thin rope over a large drop.
O, their sharp vocabulary—
the wild dogs:
their quick comprehension of divided hearts.

Horse

Here was my youth—ten years
immured in mud, wine-dark dark, entrenched.
When they came to us with the work order: A horse—
fleet of foot, wind-driven beast, *etcetera*—
in consolation for a lifetime on our bellies,
we said:
'no. Is this how we will be remembered? A *Horse?*'

We built them a fine goat instead. Something
closer to the spirit of Argos.
Odysseus, he of the oaken executive table,
wily, the hatchet man, *etcetera,* came to see me.
Told me the goat would not do. 'I'm here
to help you, to improve the quality of service,
to add value. It's an excellent goat,
fierce of eye, rampant, sharp of
tooth, *etcetera etcetera,*
but the Trojan prefers a horse
above all else. Why flatter them
with a goat so real when fantasy
is what they want?'
                                    'We have no wood
for a Horse,' I said.
                                    'Rob the graveyard,' he answered.
'The dead have no use for pine.'
'We have no time,' I told him.
                                    'Work harder,' he said.
'I have a new tool from Athena. This hammer,
you see, has tines on the back to pull nails. With this
innovation one man can pound *and* pull nails. We're
letting half of you go home.'

                    'Goodbye then, my Lord.'

'Not you,' he said. 'When this is over
                    I need you to refit the boat.'

                    'We've fixed those rotting
galleys. Made siege engines, bows and lances—
death written all over them. We've
given you shields for your bodies, metal hats
for your heads, now all you talk about
is a Horse? We could all have been home
long ago if you had fought smarter, argued
less over precedence and costume. At day's end
we put down tools and turn from this
land to the sea. Listen to the double-waved whisper
of home on the shore. The salt tongue
probes the broken tooth of homesickness, *etcetera etcetera.*

'How 'bout we build you a Fish? We
could make a very good Fish—a really
scary, mighty whale. An effigy
for the Ocean *and* we could bring
it in under budget
with the wood we have here.
                    No. You
want a Horse.
This idol of bad omen, creature of victory
and loss.

Spirit Guide

1

In the fourteenth century village of Montaillou
the spirit guide cautioned the villagers
                                    to walk carefully
with their elbows held in—
                        too much swinging
of the arms
            will knock over the ghosts
                                who shamble
from town to town
                staying overnight
                                in village churches.
Once
        in hot September, I crossed an open field—
                                        the air heavy
with heat and the first leaves
                        turning to dust, fluttering
to the ground; no, I see
                    it is a bird that moves like a leaf,
and the hot air is like a blanket
                            I want to pull over myself
                                        in this country
you'd said you'd never set foot in if they paid you.

Now I want to remember
                    instead
                        the fistfull of fear in my chest
as the cyclist
            coming up silent behind me—his laughter
at my sharp breath
                when his shadow swept over me.
                                    My mistake,

it wasn't a leaf falling
           it was a bird. Our perceptions
                      are not even that acute:
how can we perceive the heart of a man? The laughing cyclist
                  disappears over the rise
                  in the ground, ha ha ha ha.

2

In Dante's journey the ghosts
came up to him
          surprised
to see someone followed by a shadow.
In death, the ghosts are the shades
etched by the lives they'd led.
A living person may still alter the shadow
that follows him.
The things fathers do are shadows cast
in the lives of their children.
They can't be
          altered and sometimes
we meet them along the road
and we must keep our elbows in
and not flail about so as we walk
or the shades about us will begin to fall—
and we so afraid
to tumble with them.

when I was six, I wandered off from the family
campsite and climbed a desert mountain. I lost
my nerve and couldn't climb down. You came after
and like Virgil in that poem you picked me up
and slid on your back down the mountain.
Maybe I struggled against my rescue. I would

64

have found my own way down, or
maybe not—

       In that story, they fled from demons,

                              sometimes it seems

you carried me back into the arms

               of our demons—

                      your firm hand

on the back of my neck

           your own back bloody and torn by our fall.

We returned to the family.

            Each in his own world,

                     my arms

held in, careful not to knock a ghost. Yours, too, I notice.

Convict Lake

1989 Berlin

We stumble into the square below
the Brandenburg Gate.
Lenin loiters on the corner,
his chiseled forehead as fixed as ever,
but the rocks and sidewalks all around him
are moving west.

Broken Trabis line the roads
like erratic boulders left behind a glacial thaw,
while the ex-soldiers of evaporating empire
sell their medals at the curb for gasoline.

In the delirium of our new world, a German clown
with bicycle horn and floppy shoes
honks around the windswept crowd
handing balloons out to kids.
An African-American family stands
beside us as the clown hustles past, the daughter—
three years-old—tugs on his pantaloons as he goes
past. She wants a balloon.
The clown
   pauses a moment—
to look at the girl, and then the family
before he spits on the ground and turns away.

Her father, tall (he of the conquering Army),
angry fists around his video camera,
shouts, "Hey you, you . . . *Clown*. Hey!"
The German runs
    —waddles—
as fast as his shoes allow.

The shouting father follows after
videotaping as he goes.

1991 California
On a mountainside above
Convict Lake in the Sierra,
red vein of rock shattered in place
as the mountains crowd around us.

We hunch and hurry on
in the summer heat.
The way climbs higher
through scree, slag, bitterbrush.

The mountains, at their own pace,
vote with their feet:
working their way down the slope—
avalanche and earthquake—
to the dark lake below.

This is no place to hide your soul,
neither here on the mountain,
nor with the trout at lake bottom.

Last February three boys
from the nearby reform school
slid under the ice. Four
of their rescuers died with them.
EMTs and prison guards stretched out
(as we've all been told to do) flat
on the ice,
reaching for the others.
So we stretch out,

feeling the solid give way,
all going in at once in panic.

A brittle, loose geology carries us
the convict and the innocent: if
you hang back, if you rush off—
the ice underneath us
solid as a San Francisco neighborhood.

Around the corner of that rock,
secure in summer heat,
I feel a cool touch on my neck—
a breath from the snow bank
crouching there in shadowed remnant
of that glacial engine.

The Death of Lorca

The gravedigger was a prisoner himself, lucky
they didn't shoot him as well when he finished
burying the dead. They kept him busy
for the duration of the war.
He was seventeen years old, kept in a prison cell
when he wasn't digging graves. His cellmates
were a bunch of freemasons the Fascists found suspicious.
The cells were on the second floor of the Colonia.
Captain Nestares of the Fascist Army
lived on the first floor with the assassins,
a couple of housekeepers, and his girlfriend—
a young English woman named Fanny
who liked to wear the blue uniform shirt and
bright swastika of the Spanish fascist.

The executioners went by names like 'Jamuga'
and 'El Verdugo.' 'El Sevilla' shot himself dead one morning
while cleaning his gun. No one knows how many people
Captain Nestares killed. Up the road
to the killing ground, the road called the Archbishop's Road,
in an open field as big as a football stadium, are the bodies.
On August 11, mid-morning, the young gravedigger
went to the low wall where the killers left the bodies.
There were four corpses with bullets through their brains.
Two he recognized at once. They were sports heroes,
bullfighters who happened to support the left. He
knew the third, a one-legged man, a school teacher
from the next village. The fourth man was a mystery,
but he wore a loose tie about his neck, "you know,
like those ties artists wear."

Lorca's friend, the composer Manuel de Falla,
went that morning to the Government House to plead

for Lorca's life. The soldiers told him Lorca was already dead.
They grabbed the composer and led him out to the patio
where they liked to shoot people when they were in a hurry.
An officer, passing by, recognized de Falla and took him
out to the street, letting him escape. De Falla
went to Lorca's parents' house, but couldn't tell them
what he knew. Two days later a soldier came from headquarters
with a note for Lorca's family, and Lorca's last writing:
"Dear father, please give the bearer of this letter
a donation of 1,000 pasetas for the Armed Forces. Love Federico."

Choral

Homage to Brecht

Lo, if there be a miserable existence thereon
twist its neck by passionate embrace and failure.
Carry forth, O Zion, those tender feelings crosshatched
in tank treads, show us again
the body plowed under, the glazed beauty
of bone and that evocative stillness. Rev
your language, run it through your gears,
splinter me with the teeth of naming. Laws,
nailed one   through the fist,   nailing two

                                        the wrong
turn, run down crossing your friend, fucking

                                        three
his wife breathing the dust of better places
while squandering this one. The trees
weep, even the prostitutes are prostitutes.
The birds lift the sky—only the sky.

The Bridge

In 1948, Time *magazine writer and one-time poet Whittaker Chambers named State Department deputy Alger Hiss as a member of the Communist Party and a spy for the Soviet Union. Richard Nixon was the prosecuting attorney in the subsequent investigation that ended Hiss's career. As material evidence of Chambers's good character a copy of the famous Zukofsky edition of* Poetry *magazine of 1931, in which Chambers appeared along with W. C. Williams, Carl Rakosi, Charles Reznikoff, and others, was entered into the court record.*

. . . And I went on
        eating it. It was
that good.

                Yeah, haw,
                that's good, Mr.
                Nixon. Now
                about these poets.

It's this book
entered in
evidence, by
Chambers in the
Alger Hiss case—

                One commie
                fingering
                another.

Yeah, you got that
right. Hoover
put me on it.

This book?

This uh, poetry
book, edited
by a russki
jew name of
Zukofsky. Why,
the whole thing
is full of
Ruzznikoffs, *Carlos*
Williams, Raskoski—

Is this our
national—

'the [expletive deleted], still itself
among the [expletive].'

our
national literature?

But look—

is this what—

Look,

we've come to?

Longfellow, it ain't—

No, sir—

but I never uh, I never
liked that crap.

                  Ah, no, I never—

You see how clean
this [expletive deleted]
looks here.

                  Well—

And it says:
"The Bridge
In a cloud bones of steel."

Oh!   Oh!
Ah!   Wah haa
That [expletive]
hurt.

Swimming Pool Exorcism

Edie Sedgwick haunts the deep end
of the suburban pool—
and at night, from under the diving board,
the moaning of all divers rises
to the moon.

The priest sets his chair
by the pool, listening
to Edie recite all the lines to *Ciao Manhattan*.

She rants at Andy
and boredom, or boredom
and Andy, if you prefer.

Under the pale green glow of swimming pool lamps
the stars reflect on the oily broken surface of the toddler motel.

Forget speed. Fashion kills, she says.
The silicone would have done it
if the heroin hadn't.
It's the tragedy of life before
cosmetic surgery: you might take your guns
without butter now,
but it's hard to say, father, that meaner is any leaner.

He isn't listening. He's deep into his own recitation,
his fingers worry the wrapper from a Jolly Rancher
he's discovered in his pocket.
After a couple turns of the neck
like a pepper grinder over an L.A. salad, he evicts
the ghost from the pool then wanders on
to the bar to spend his fee.

Under the pale green glow of swimming pool lamps
the stars reflect on the oily broken surface of the toddler motel.

Hummer Apocalypse

The various accessories—
7 seals and 7 horns—were
previewed
in the press kit. St John
forgot to mention
the Beast's 7 m.p.g.

April

April is four fingers
deep in the mud,
the wet and wind-burnt
birth of the world
that finds you
in any doorway
where you are.
                    There, put
in memory of place, the
one or two you have—
clues to the riddle
the world gives you as April.
The smell of rain
on railroad ties,
damp black stone,
red cedar, the yellowed leaves
of last autumn.

Eurydice's Song

Where do we go
in despair
in hunger for
the forgotten spark
in darkness?

          Osiris,
Lazarus, we know
the gift of sleep
and the waking chant
of sunrise.
O let me rest here,
splinter of light.

Always
the voice, the shadow of your back
before me
retreating
into the dawn
the light that clothes me,
discloses me,
in flesh. I am nothing
without the light,
this body.
I remember what
wraps me in light.
And still you go on
calling me after
and I, reluctant flesh,
follow.

Will I regret
this time of death

as I did the mistakes
of life? Death,
will you
call me back in your turn?
and you, life, retreating
from me, can you in your song—
the self-glory of your own
creation—can you feel
the shade that follows you?

My awakening,
morning earth in my
lungs, the wind of my voice
in this throat,
calling out to you,
to turn you, the
force of my desire.

You have to have a good memory to be bitter

Otis Redding, d. December 1967, Madison, Wisconsin

Walking by Lake Monona
the evening on the trees,
like yesterday evening,
though that was different.
The trees standing in rain-slick
leaves already out and branching
over the water.
                 From the shore,
the distance reaches, like the trees,
for that same sweet breath of eternity
Otis found at the end of a whistle:
a few drops of spring rain
cold down the collar of your coat
and the bass rumbles the changes
playing out there on the horizon.

Extra

All along the light rushing toward us
at the end of the tunnel
was mounted upon
a giant eclair. In California,
the Hollywood extra thinks again
about his one movie. It was
a pirate film and Errol Flynn
ran him and a dozen other pirates
through with his cutlass. The extra
thought he'd grimaced with great dash:
'I am being stabbed. I am a pirate
among pirates, being skewered like big kabob . . .
or like Hector, like Hector the noble loser of Troy
(except I was born in Greece,
but that doesn't matter; here in America
I can be a Greek
killed by Errol Flynn—just like anyone else).'
That was sixty years of shipbuilding ago.
Now, the old man
takes a break
from his morning-long project
of opening a can of dog food—
remembering Flynn's happy smile.
"I should'a clocked that prick," he thinks.
"I should'a cleaned his clock."

Willy McGee

Too many people wept for Achilles
when he stumbled out of the pit
of blood, Ulysses shed a tear—
but Ulysses was always the canny one.
Who weeps for Ted Williams? Or
the last days of Willy McGee? Steady
Bob Welch pitching
a last no hitter in Cincinnati—
the home town that refused to
draft him?
              Dear Mr. McGee,
will you please sign this baseball
and tell me how you continue—
how to go on in summer light?
The curve of the pop fly
steeper than the Italianate arch
in the summer garden, the rough
table and bench set with my parents'
bitter meal and my mother
groaned out loud and my father
wept. Before we part, the sunlight reaches
in hazy shafts through the trellis. I hear
the desultory birdsong when the crowd
is silent. Will you sign this ball
and retire that side, open
all the dead letters,
tell me how to hammer
a knuckleball from Candeotti?
This baseball isn't for me—
it's for my older brother
who became a vampire this year
and no longer needs this information.

And at times it seems
I only hear him now as a faint
voice—soft as the noise
of the grass growing in the
places of summer where nobody walks.

Lamentations

Homage to Vallejo

The ice-cream truck sings the little
song of my death. In a cloud
the Lord in his anger clothes
the daughter of Zion. In the pocket
of an old jacket: lint, handkerchief,
death. I have beaten death with a shovel
and a rope, though my death has done
me no harm. Still, it remains,
undismayed. In Pennsylvania,
the car noses its way through the fog.
Even after my death is dead I
went on beating it; tomorrow,
remembering all the times I carried
it, cupped in my hands, blowing
warm breath over its beaked little face.

Moth light nostalghia

For J. Gluckstern

Translucency comes of the unresolved antimony of the two currents, of the vital swerve into and away from the core of the original.

—George Steiner, *After Babel*

The light flickers on the rockface—
a retinal moon working against
time: petroglyphs of bison,
hunting shadows on the wall.

J. and I followed the track
down the canyon. A national park
named after fossils. We were talking
about that movie where Tarkovsky

struggles to keep a candle lit
crossing the puddled, drafty
floor of an empty Roman bath.
In Boulder, Brakhage got up

to introduce *Andrei Rublev*—four
hours of fifteenth-century Russia
watching the paint dry with the icon
painter while waiting for the next wave

of Tatars to show up
and introduce the next film. Brakhage's
Roman Numeral series for instance:
black screen in a dark

theater: long rhythm wait to a candle
flash of red—sudden as the inspiration
of a petroglyph—the scene flashed
across the inside of my eye.

Far off the sound of a clattering
antelope at twenty-four frames per second.
Film. What an artifact. Scratches—
moth wings fluttering against a wall.

The Soviet landed in Las Vegas, "The proletarian
capital of the world." The entire country
simply camping out with no architecture,
no culture . . . the usual complaints. It's only

fitting then that when they met
in Teluride and the Russian
saw the American's work, Tarkovsky
told Brakhage he was full of shit.

At the bottom of the park the
moon rise reflects off the confluence
of the canyon-carving rivers Green
and Yampa and shines upon

the cliff-face opposite our camp. When
you trace the pale line
of geologic disturbance evident
in the separate species

of green plant growing side
by side along that line (each
in its most favorable soil), tell me—

how are plants native or
                                    alien?

Seed carried out of the steppe
in a blackbird's craw? Or stuffed
in the hold of a famine ship? We end here—
speaking English in the dinosaur's basement

watching the glyphs on that far wall working.

Wheels

The bodies weighed so little that any Indian could carry them from house to house in his arms or on his shoulders. They carried them wrapped in white sheets through the streets and squares, the Indians falling to their knees and making reverence with groans and tears, and many Spaniards taking off their caps.

—Garcilaso de la Vega, quoted in
The Conquest of the Incas, by John Hemming

The bus kneels and rolls out
its tongue, a smug cat lapping up
the woman in the wheelchair.

The platform ascends
and she rides in
her left hand nudging the joystick
of her motorized chair.

She's got her wheels.
It's important to have wheels.
When the Spanish found out
the Inca had never discovered the wheel
they felt justified in killing everybody.
You move or they kill you.

Samuel Pepys wrote more about
his carriage and its fine upholstery
than his wife, or his politics.
The cruising up and down St. James Park
of Restoration English nobility
was political culture: who's driving what—
how many horses—did you see the shit
on the footman's shoes? They were footmen

because they didn't have wheels of their own.
We've been waiting since the Inquisition
for Kerouac to pull out of Lowell
and roll past the stop sign, past the all-night wafer-thin
promises of the Rites of Man, the slap-me-stupid
sing-along of the hero out on a mainline solo
with the needle pushing empty
but we didn't care. We didn't care
because we all went along for
the chorus
                    our bellies soft
with that weird fucking diner food—
burnt strips of bacon and could I get some more
of that fine coffee, darling, when you get a chance?

Yeah, you get you some wheels
and we'll have some good times.
                                        Late at night
the conquistador-hero lies awake listening
to the new freeway.
The shining exit at Broadway
and Atahualpa. Under the sickle moon, the scent of diesel
wafts from the semis proceeding down the valley.
The conquistador looks from his window to see
a figure stagger into the minimall parking lot
into the midnight glare of the arc light.
A tall ghost drifts by the phosphorescent
storefront, moaning as it goes.
                                        The hem
of its white shroud
trails through radiator-green puddles.

It is the Inca, stumbling
over the concrete planters,
carrying his ancestor's bones across his shoulders.

The unraveling cloth of the
mummified corpse covers them both.
He sobs and cries out as he goes.

Wim Wenders vs. the Wolfman

Desire is an engine of metamorphosis

The blind man sets Frankenstein's monster down
with a cup of coffee and a cigar—
though the monster is skittish
and flinches when the old man strikes the match.

Wenders' Angel falls to earth
picks himself up and walks over to the kiosk.
His first desire as a mortal:
a cup of joe and a cigarette.

Angels are monstrous
and we desire them
though they bite back
with desires of their own:
Her eyes may be dark,
the needle a sweet
black nipple of sugar—
how good that road of dark change.

Boris Karloff, played by
William Henry Pratt, inhabited
the role of Frankenstein's monster so well
he could never shake it.
Children, dogs, and Hollywood agents
cringed away in horror
at the creature and his lesson.

We are only the clumsy servants
of desire. Blind and Mr. Magoo-like
we have the very thing of creation

seated in our kitchen while we struggle
with a cheese grater.
"Here you are. Let me cut you a piece of bread—
Oh! I'm sorry. The knife slipped.
Did it cut you, my big friend?
Let's wash that cut in this tub of bleach—
Wait, leaving so soon?
You haven't finished your coffee."

The angels of the Lord stop by.
They are terrible
in their changeless desire.
They're on their way
to blast Sodom and want
a coffee and a fag. You don't smoke
and only have de-caf.
Surely, the Lord will smite you down—
if only you knew it.
                    Your angels insist
they don't want any bread, so
you give them oranges—feeling
your eyebrows singe as they
take them from your hands.
In this fire, you recognize
here is something outside the human:
a fulcrum to move planets.

KEVIN DUCEY's work has appeared in *River City, Malahat, Elixir,* and *Crab Orchard Review,* among others. He was the recipient of a Wisconsin Arts Board grant in 2000 and received an MFA from the University of Notre Dame. He currently lives in Madison, Wisconsin.